THE MIDDLE YEARS

SASQUATCH SENIOR COMMUNITY
BOOK 4

PATRICK TALMADGE

HANGAR 1 PUBLISHING

Captain Jimmy was born in 1955, near Ormond Beach, Florida, into a family of physicians, but when Jimmy was 14 years old (1969), his father bought him a boat, which helped him fall in love with the water and fishing.

1

JIMMY MEETS GU

Jimmy decided, like any 14-year-old boy would do in his position, to take the brand new 18 hp boat motor off his heavy fishing boat and put it on a 10-foot-long flat bottom aluminum john boat for some real speed. Of course, he wouldn't dare ask his dad because his dad would lecture him on the dangers of going too fast in a boat out on the ocean. Well, Jimmy wasn't crazy enough to try his speedboat idea out on the ocean; he was going to try it on the Tomoka River, where the water was smoother, and his dad wouldn't catch him.

The motor was heavier than Jimmy expected, and he needed a wheelbarrow to bring it over to the smaller, lighter boat. Mounting the motor wasn't too hard, but the motor was so heavy Jimmy needed to move the gas tank, battery, and all the loose gear to the bow of the boat to keep the boat's front end from flying. He also needed to use an extension for the motor tiller so he could sit towards the front of the boat to help keep the bow down. If Jimmy's dad, or any other adult for that matter, had seen Jimmy's setup, they would have stopped him. As luck or fate would have it, his dad was at work, no other adults were around, and he was a 14-year-old boy with a plan and no supervision, so the plan went forward. It went forward really fast, too.

Jimmy knew the boat would go faster than his heavy fishing boat, but he wasn't expecting the little flat-bottom boat to go as fast as it did. Even after moving all the extra weight and himself forward, the bow still wanted to lift if he went too fast, so Jimmy was forced to back off the throttle a bit. The boat was fantastic to drive, and Jimmy was glad he used the big gas tank so he could play longer. After making sure everything was working well and he had dialed the speed down enough to be safe, Jimmy headed upriver. Jimmy cruised for about 25 minutes when he came around a corner fast and saw a boat by the shore, so he began to slow down.

As Jimmy went by the other boat, still going a bit too fast, he saw KO, the boat pilot, and a giant ape-like thing staring at him as he flew by. KO and Wally (Wally is what KO calls him, but his name given to him by his people is Gu) were going up the river collecting fish from the people living along the river. Many of the people living on the river working and dealing with KO knew of Wally. Wally was only 11 years old, but he was already over 6-foot-tall, with dark reddish-brown fur, and it was very hard to hide in an open boat during the daytime.

With the fact that Jimmy was going too fast, he had unexpectedly seen a big hairy ape thing in a boat. He was in the middle of a curve in a narrow river channel, which led to him running aground. Jimmy was going so fast when he hit the bank both he and the boat ended up 30 feet from the shoreline into the brush. Luckily, Jimmy flew further than the boat, so it didn't land on him.

If a camera had filmed the incident, you could have made money showing it to people. The look on Jimmy's face when he saw Wally was pure shock and bewilderment. The look on his face when he hit the bank was no less of a shock but much more amazing to watch. Luckily, Jimmy was young, light, and in good shape because when the boat came to a stop, he didn't. KO guessed Jimmy did at least 3 cartwheels before he landed. Jimmy's luck was still holding because he landed in the thick brush, which cushioned his fall.

KO and Wally watched Jimmy speed by, hit the bank, and fly like a tumbler in a circus. Jimmy didn't land much like a cat, but with a splat, because the bush he landed on covered a shallow pool. Jimmy stood up immediately, unhurt physically, but his pride might be a bit bruised, thought KO as he drove his boat over to the sight of the wreck.

Jimmy was so upset about crashing the boat he'd forgotten about seeing Wally until KO drove his boat to the bank where Jimmy had crashed. KO called out to ask if Jimmy was hurt, and when Jimmy turned to answer KO, he saw Wally, then he stumbled backwards and fell right back into the pool, which caused Wally to burst out laughing. Once Jimmy realized Wally was laughing and would not attack, he started laughing himself as it dawned on him how funny he must look lying in a muddy pool.

When Wally first saw Jimmy, he was immediately drawn to him. Wally had been around humans for over 5 years and recognized that Jimmy was a kid, but it was his first time around a human near his age. Sandy was a little girl, and the rest of the humans he knew were adults, so Jimmy was the first human Wally had been with that was a kid like him, and he had a boat, too.

KO called out to Jimmy again to make sure he was OK. Jimmy answered, still lying on his back, laughing in the small pool, that he was OK. KO let Jimmy know that Wally would be coming over to help him, and he said that Wally was not dangerous at all. Anyone the least bit observant would have realized Wally was by no means angry or dangerous because he was still laughing so hard, he was on his knees holding on to the side of the boat so he wouldn't fall over. Jimmy was still lying on his back, but he could hear Wally laughing, and the thought of an ape laughing at him made Jimmy laugh even harder.

After Wally and Jimmy stopped laughing enough that KO could talk to them, he let Jimmy know that Wally would be coming over to help him drag the boat out of the bushes back to the river. Jimmy had pulled himself up to a sitting position and watched as Wally stepped out of the boat and walked effortlessly through the thick brush toward him. Wally was still laughing a little bit, which helped Jimmy to feel relaxed, but Wally's over 6-foot height, large build, and the fact he was totally covered with fur was a bit intimidating to Jimmy, so he was feeling a bit nervous.

Wally walked over to Jimmy, who was still sitting in the pool, but he stopped about 5 feet away so he wouldn't scare Jimmy. Wally knew he was scary to humans when they first met him, so he stopped a few feet away from Jimmy, held out his large hand, and said "up" to Jimmy.

Jimmy looked at Wally and said, "You can talk?"

Wally looked down at Jimmy, shook his head up and down, and said, "A little bit."

Jimmy was staring wide-eyed at Wally and said, "Oh my God, this is incredible. I can't believe you can talk." Then Jimmy held up his hand so Wally could help him up.

From that moment on, KO would say that these two were inseparable and would be lifetime best friends.

Wally helped Jimmy stand, and for the longest time after Jimmy was standing up, the two of them stood looking at each other. It's not like they were sizing each other up. Both were just incredibly curious about the other. Jimmy wasn't afraid at all; he was marveling at the height of Wally and how cool it was that he was totally covered with fur.

Jimmy looked at Wally and then pointed to himself and said, "My name is Jimmy. What is your name?"

Wally looked at Jimmy, smiled, pointed at himself, and said, "My people call me Gu, but my human friends call me Wally."

"I like Wally", said Jimmy, "it is easier than Gu for me to remember," and then he laughed again.

KO saw that the two were not having any problems getting along, but like all boys their age, they needed a bit of encouragement to get the job at hand done, so he reminded them they needed to get that boat off dry land and back into the water before the boat forgot how to swim.

KO's remark got the boys moving, but it made them laugh even more than they already were. After Jimmy picked up the things that had flown out of the boat when it went aground, Wally single-handedly pulled the boat back to the river. Being over 6-foot-tall, weighing over 300 pounds, and stronger than four grown men combined made doing heavy lifting easy for Wally.

The bow of the boat had been bent up a little bit, but the boat was relatively undamaged because it had landed in the brush. KO showed Wally how to straighten the bent bow so that it looked like it had never been damaged. Wally's hand strength was more than enough to bend aluminum, and when he was done, it was nearly impossible to tell it had been bent.

After they loaded up the boat gear that had flown out in the crash, they tried the boat motor. Luckily, the motor started right up, and other than having a broken shear pin on the prop, nothing else was wrong with the boat. Luckily, Jimmy had a pack of sheer pins in the boat's toolbox, so his boat was ready to go after he replaced it.

After KO checked Jimmy's boat to make sure it was safe to drive, he suggested Jimmy follow him down to his Marina so they could talk. Wally thought it was a great idea that Jimmy come down and talk, but Wally wanted to ride with Jimmy because his weight would help keep the bow of Jimmy's boat down. KO laughed because he knew Wally liked Jimmy and wanted to ride with him more than he was worried about the bow rising. Before KO could say yes or no, Jimmy piped up and said it would be a great idea for Wally to ride with him and keep the bow down so he could see better.

KO laughed and told the boys to keep the speed down, your life vests on, and he would meet them at his Tomaka Boat Marina. KO knew the boys needed time alone to get to know one another, so he decided on sending them ahead. Also, if they got into trouble, he wouldn't be too far behind them.

2

JIMMY AND GU BECOME SECRET BEST FRIENDS

Jimmy and Wally's first boat ride set the stage for their lifelong friendship. Wally was unusual for Sasquatch in that he liked water, especially when he was on boats, and like Jimmy, he had fishing fever also. One would have thought that since Wally fell into the Tomoka river when he was 5 years old, and KO found him clinging to a log floating in the river, he would hate water. For some reason, Wally loved the water, which helped forge the bond with Jimmy.

Jimmy learned that while Wally grew and got older, he would have more problems talking. As it turns out, as Sasquatch get older their vocal cords become stiffer, and speech is more difficult. With all the time Jimmy and Wally spent together, Jimmy made it his goal to learn many of the Sasquatch words, which were easier for Wally to say, and he learned their Sasquatch sign language as well. Jimmy liked using sign language because it was silent and could be useful for fishing and hunting. One of the best uses of Sasquatch sign language was when Jimmy was around humans, but there were Sasquatch in the jungle around them, and he needed to communicate with them.

On any given day when Jimmy wasn't in school, he could be found in his boat fishing with Wally. The two boys wanted to spend all their time fishing and floating around. Summers were the two best friend's favorite time. They could spend all day together. Back in the 1970's kids had much more freedom than they do now, and it wasn't unusual for kids to be out all day. The biggest problem was Jimmy couldn't tell anyone about his secret best friend, so everyone thought Jimmy was a loner without friends.

Jimmy told his parents he was working with KO, at his Tomoka Boat Marina to earn extra money to afford fishing tackle and extras for his boat. Wally would meet him there, and the two of them would head out into the swamp or go fishing. Wally was getting so big they couldn't spend much time in Jimmy's boat on the Halifax River or fishing offshore because people would see him. Since Wally couldn't hide his size, they spent most of their time together exploring and fishing up the Tomoka River.

3

JIMMY MEETS COOPER

One day when the boys were boating up the river, Wally saw Cooper fishing in a small channel off the river and asked Jimmy to turn around, so he could introduce them to one another. Wally warned Jimmy to keep the speed super slow and stop at least 100-feet away from Cooper's boat. Cooper had taught Wally to always approach another person's boat slowly, then stop with enough room between boats so you don't disturb whatever it is they might be doing. That was standard river courtesy, and it always worked except one time.

The one exception using that rule was one morning when the boys came upon a boat with two fishermen, whom Wally thought was Cooper and his friend. It was foggy on the river, so the boys couldn't really tell for sure if it was Cooper or not, even from within 100 feet. After waiting a couple of minutes for the people in the boat to signal them, the boys got curious and slowly motored towards the two men in the boat. When they were within 20 feet, Wally held his hand up to tell Jimmy to stop the boat. Wally turned around towards Jimmy, with his hand covering his mouth because he was laughing hard, and pointed into the boat.

Jimmy let the boat drift closer so he could get a better look into the boat, and instantly started laughing. Inside the boat was two fishermen who were passed out drunk, with empties covering the bottom of the boat. Obviously, these two had been out fishing when the drinking caught up to them last night. They were lucky no gator or panther found them passed out and ate them, plus it is very dangerous to drink and boat. Before Jimmy could stop him, Wally started saying in a slightly loud voice that it is not safe to drink while drinking. A 'slightly loud voice' for a Sasquatch can wake the dead, or in this case, the dead drunk, and when it did, the sight was hysterical.

Wally's voice boomed loud, and the boat the passed-out fisherman was in might have even been vibrating pretty heavily as both men sat up like they had been shocked. Jimmy had drifted their boat next to the drunk guy's boat, so when the drunk guys came to, opened their eyes, and sat up, Wally was looking directly down at them.

The boat the fishermen were in had drifted up against some thick brush next to shore and gotten hung up, which was a good thing because when they saw Wally, they screamed and jumped out the other side of their boat. The men climbed over the brush and were last seen running across the marsh. It took Wally a good 15 minutes to stop laughing, and Jimmy wasn't much better off. Wally and Jimmy still laugh at that story, but back then, they decided not to tell Cooper, KO, or anyone else for that matter, to avoid any possible trouble for scaring the guys.

Wally had Jimmy follow the normal river courtesy in case Cooper was trying to catch a gator or large catfish and needed silence. Cooper only took 15 or 20 seconds to signal the boys over. Cooper had been engrossed in hauling up his blue crab traps and hadn't seen the boys at first. Jimmy and Wally started laughing because they both had thought of the two drunk guys when Cooper didn't instantly respond, so they were still chuckling when they pulled aside Cooper's boat.

Cooper looked at the boys laughing in their boat and said, "I can guess from the juvenile laughter and antics this is Jimmy?"

Cooper's remark only made the boys laugh even more, so he suggested they follow him up the river to his houseboat after he dropped his crab trap again.

"If you two can settle down by the time we get to my place, I'm cooking up a pot of these blue crab," Cooper said. "No laughing when eating the crab because it gets messy," Cooped added, then sped away in his boat.

True to his word, Cooper had a pot of blue crabs on a burner when they arrived. Cooper took the pot that was on the burner off and set it on a steel mesh grate, then poured the contents of the pot onto the grating. A good three dozen steaming cooked crabs were now cooling on the grating while Cooper pulled the blue crabs he had just caught out of the basket and placed them into the pot. Once he had filled the pot with crabs, Cooper placed the pot back onto the burner and filled the pot with water and his special spices.

While the new crabs were cooking and the cooked crabs were cooling, Cooper cleaned up his work area, changed his shirt, grabbed three plates, and suggested the boys try some of his freshly caught and cooked crab. Cooper hadn't finished asking before the boys stood and headed to the cooling crabs. After tasting his first bite of Cooper's special blue crab, Jimmy decided he needed to start catching these and adding them to his diet.

While the boys ate like teenage boys do, Cooper learned about Jimmy and what the two boys had been doing. After their fourth crab, the boys told Cooper about the two drunk guys in the boat

Wally had scared. The boys started laughing but made sure to not have mouthfuls of crab, and Cooper got quite a laugh out of the story.

Cooper suggested that Wally take Jimmy up the river and introduce him to some of the river people that Wally knew so they would know Jimmy was someone they could trust. Cooper also suggested that if Jimmy became a doctor like some of his family did, he could do Doctor houseboat calls up the river? Jimmy promised he would do that 'if' he became a doctor, but he was looking forward to meeting Cooper and Wally's friends. Cooper asked if Wally had taken Jimmy to his village yet, and Wally suggested Jimmy needed to meet a few more river people before he was subjected to meeting his Sasquatch troupe.

"You might be right about getting this city boy a bit more acclimated to river life before he meets the real river people," said Cooper with a huge smile. "I was river born, river raised, and meeting Wally's family was a bit unnerving, to say the least," Cooper added. "You two river rats better keep your wake low and the eyes open on this river, or people will find out about Wally and his kind," was the advice Cooper finished with.

Jimmy's family were doctors, and he was raised in an upper-middle-class family with inside plumbing, a nanny, and a silver spoon in his mouth, so teased Cooper. Going to Wally's, or as his people call him, Gu's village, would be a bit of a shock. Jimmy admitted that going to Wally's village was a bit scary, but only because everyone they will be huge, and not too many of them know English like Wally. Jimmy told Cooper he was learning as many Sasquatch words and sign language as possible before he visited to make it easier. Cooper agreed that Jimmy's idea was smart and suggested he and Wally practice a lot. After the boys had their fill of crab, they headed out to the boat and continued back up the river to explore.

4

LANIE COLLINS IS WALLY'S HUMAN GRANDMA

Twenty minutes after leaving Cooper's, Wally had Jimmy turn the boat into a small cove off the main river, then pull up to a dock. Jimmy saw a definite change in Wally. He got excited and acted more like a little kid going into a toy store than a sasquatch going up to a human house without them knowing you were coming. For all his size and power, Wally knocked on the door with the gentleness of a small child, but if he'd been a Labrador dog, his tail would have been wagging out of control. He was so excited. As soon as the door opened, Jimmy saw the reason. A lady that looked like an angel opened the door, and Wally almost melted.

The angel lady looked at Wally and said, "OH, my sweet little Gu, how are you, little one? Are you hungry?" "You look starving. You better sit down and let Lanie Collins get you something to eat." Lanie added after she fawned all over Wally, or as she calls him Gu, which is his family-given name, and ushered him inside.

Once Wally entered the door, Lanie noticed Jimmy standing outside, saying, "OH my Gu brought a friend, and he is a human."

"This is a big and monumental day for Sasquatch and humans," she added, then held out her hand to Jimmy to bring him in as well.

Once both boys were inside, Lanie introduced herself to Jimmy. When Jimmy told her who he was, she was very impressed. She told Jimmy it was nice to see one of the city kids explore the river, especially with Gu, so he could get an idea of what the simple river folk are like. Lanie told Jimmy she knew his family were doctors and had even seen Jimmy's grandfather and father as their patients a few times over the years.

Lanie makes Gu's favorite treat in the world, blueberry hush puppies. Wally loves Lanie like a grandma, and she adores him, commenting how big he has gotten, and must be her hush puppies making him so big.

While the boys ate their fill of hush puppies, which was enough for six regular people, which for teenage boys was expected, Lanie told Jimmy how she met Gu. Lanie explained that she came home late one night and heard a sound in her shed by the dock. She grabbed a light and her shotgun, thinking it might be a varmint, and looked in carefully. What she saw shocked her, and she stepped back in surprise. She almost shot her shotgun.

What she saw was a giant ape huddled in the pile of straw back in the corner. When Lanie gained her wits and secured the shotgun better, she noticed the ape wasn't coming towards her; it was actually crouched down and looked distressed. Lanie held her lamp higher and saw the ape was a female, and she was pregnant. She was not only pregnant. She appeared to be in labor, but not normal labor. Lanie could see the ape was not having an easy birth and began worrying, so she moved closer to see better.

It was obvious the ape was in pain, and something was wrong, so Lanie looked at the ape, held her hands out to the ape, then rubbed her belly, and made a crying face and sound. The ape looked at Lanie, touched her own belly, and cried, so Lanie knew the ape was in trouble. Lanie put her lamp and shotgun down and slowly stepped towards the ape with her open, empty hands held out. The ape did not make any aggressive moves or noises, so Lanie felt the ape knew she was there to help.

After Lanie was able to touch the ape and examine her condition, she realized the ape was in labor, but the baby was a possible breach birth, and Lanie needed to act immediately, or both the mom and baby could be lost. Lanie held the ape's hand, looked into its eyes, and said she would be right back. Lanie left the apes' side and went into her house to get the things she needed to help with the birth. When Lanie returned, she could tell the ape was in pain and needed to hurry. Lanie was born on a farm here in the south, and this wasn't her first breach birth. It was, although, her first ape breach birth.

"I won't bore you with all the details, but the birth was successful for both mom and baby." Said Lanie. "In fact, that mom still visits me, along with some of the other women in Gu's troupe, as well as that breach birth baby." She added. "Ha, ha, ha, that baby is my little Gu," Lanie said, then hugged Gu.

Wally/Gu looked like a little boy getting hugs from his favorite grandmother. Except he was a huge Sasquatch, which was cute but also funny. Now Jimmy understood Wally's love for Lanie, and Jimmy could attest she was a fantastic person and a wonderful grandma. There was no doubt Lanie was going to be another lifelong friend for Jimmy as well.

When the boys had their fill of hush puppies, Lanie took them outside to show them what was happening. Jimmy was amazed at what he saw. There were three female Sasquatch with babies outside on the side deck. Lanie also showed them the garden the Sasquatch built so she could grow more corn for her hush puppies. Turns out Wally isn't the only Sasquatch that likes them.

Jimmy was sure he ate at least 25 of them, so he understood why the Sasquatch wanted to build a big garden, so she could make more. Lanie explained that since she helped Gu's mother, the Sasquatch have been her friends and helpers.

Wally introduced Jimmy to the Sasquatch that were there so they would know him as a friend of the Sasquatch when they meet in the future, even if Wally isn't with him. Jimmy was amazed at how well the Sasquatch worked and played around Lanie's house. Obviously, the Sasquatch knew it was a safe place, and they helped to take care of Lanie's home and yard as a thank you. Jimmy knew he would be back many times, even without Wally.

When it was time to go, Lanie had words of wisdom for the boys. She told them to "mind your manners, show your respect, and don't make a wake on the river." "If you follow these rules, you will not have many problems on the river or in your lives." Lanie added then she gave both boys hugs and sent them on their way.

5

JIMMY VISITS WALLY'S SASQUATCH VILLAGE

One day, when Wally and Jimmy were traveling up the Tomoka River, Wally decided it was time for Jimmy to meet his people, so he directed Jimmy to his village. Before they got there Wally explained that only a few people had ever been to his village, so his people might be a bit nervous. Wally instructed Jimmy to stay close by his side until they met his father, who is also the leader of their village. Once his father greets Jimmy, then the rest of the village will relax and accept him into the village as a family member.

Wally showed Jimmy a secret channel off the main Tomoka river, that was hidden by a floating log covered with brush and vines. KO had built the movable log to block the entrance into the channel that led to the Sasquatch, so no one would accidentally find the Sasquatch, while hunting or exploring. Wally showed Jimmy how to untie the log and float it away, so the boat could enter the small channel and then pull it closed again.

The channel was just barely wide enough for the boat, but

after 300 feet the channel opened into a wide lagoon with a sandy beach on one side. Wally had Jimmy park the boat at the beach. The beach was clean and showed no sign that anyone or anything was near, except for a well-worn trail that led from the beach into the dense brush. After Jimmy shut the boat down and Wally had tied it to a tree, the boys headed down the trail led by Wally.

Jimmy would later say walking down that trail with Wally was the scariest thing he'd ever done. Here he was, walking down a dark trail deep in the swamp, following an 8-foot-tall Sasquatch, and preparing to meet a whole village of Sasquatch. Although he had known Wally for months and met other Sasquatch, he had never been alone with so many that had not been near humans. Wally assured Jimmy that everything would be fine as long as he didn't move too quickly at first. Jimmy was so nervous he didn't notice the grin on Wally's face, or he would have figured he was being pranked.

The trail from the beach opened into a large clearing with a huge mound with a rock wall around it in the center of the clearing. As Wally and Jimmy climbed the ramp up to the top of the mound, Jimmy estimated the mound to be 10 feet tall. A stone wall encircled the complete mound at the top of the mound. The wall was also about 10 feet, and about 15 feet from the edge of the mound. The 15-foot area from the mound's edge to the wall was a walking area used as an open area to guard the wall. Not that the Sasquatch needed to be guarded from anything, thought Jimmy.

As Jimmy and Wally entered the opening in the wall into the village, Wally once advised Jimmy not to move too quickly at first, which made Jimmy tense up a bit more. Once they entered the wall opening, Jimmy could see mounds along the inside of the wall, which he knew were the houses for the Sasquatch. When they were noticed, the boys were no more than ten steps inside the wall.

Much to Jimmy's horror, all sorts of loud calls rang out from the Sasquatch he could see around the village. It only got worse for Jimmy, as dozens of the adult Sasquatch suddenly ran towards Wally and Jimmy. As Jimmy was about to scream, he saw at least 20 young Sasquatch of all sizes outrun the adults and were only seconds from reaching Jimmy. Jimmy has no memory of how he got there, but the next thing he knew, he was standing on Wally's shoulders. Jimmy would swear Wally picked him up and put him there, but Wally would tell a different story.

Wally couldn't tell the real story of what happened that day without laughing so hard he was crying. Wally says that when Jimmy saw all the yelling and screaming Sasquatch running for them, Jimmy literally climbed him like a tree and stood on his shoulders. It happened so fast that Wally was caught off guard, and so were the Sasquatch running towards them. Once the Sasquatch running towards them saw that Jimmy was standing on Wally's shoulders, they stopped dead in their tracks. It took less than 2 seconds for the laughter to start. Wally was sure the young Sasquatch started laughing first, but within moments, the whole troupe in the village was laughing.

Jimmy regained composure and jumped from Wally's shoulders to the ground. The scene before him looked like a war zone with bodies lying all over the ground. The difference between these bodies and ones in a war zone was that these bodies were alive and laughing so hard they couldn't do anything but sit and lay on the ground. As Jimmy was surveying the hysterically laughing Sasquatch around the village, a large gray-haired Sasquatch stepped out of a mound home and slowly crossed the clearing.

Jimmy immediately guessed that this was Wally's father, the troupe's leader. By the way he was walking, Jimmy could tell he was friendly because he had a big smile on his face as he walked amongst his troupe, who were still lying around laughing. By the time Wally's dad reached Jimmy and Wally, most of the troupe were just chuckling. Wally stood and gave his dad a big hug. Wally was now almost his father's size, and weeks ago, he said he was expected to grow much bigger than his dad or the other male Sasquatch. If all things worked out, then Wally would be the troupe leader someday, but for now, he was just a kid teasing his best friend, who happened to be human.

Wally's dad looked down at Jimmy and gently pet, then kissed Jimmy's head. Jimmy was frozen while Wally's dad was standing over him, so when the giant Sasquatch bent down to kiss the top of Jimmy's head, he couldn't move.

As soon as Wally's dad kissed Jimmy's head, the troupe, including Wally, burst into loud, uncontrolled laughter once again. Wally's dad smiled down at Jimmy, let out a loud laugh, then strolled off still laughing. When Wally could stop laughing, he explained that his dad was teasing Jimmy. Wally explained that that is how the adult Sasquatch greets the young Sasquatch, and that he used to tease KO by doing the same thing. Jimmy now understood how fun and sensitive the Sasquatch was.

Once everyone in the troupe settled down enough, they came up to say hi to Wally and meet Jimmy. The young Sasquatch were so cute, and Wally made a point to remind them to be gentle with Jimmy because he was just human. It took Jimmy a few seconds to realize Wally was teasing him. Although even a 4-year-old Sasquatch is stronger than a grown human, but they are very gentle and aware of their superior strength.

After greeting everyone, Wally showed Jimmy the village. What stood out the most and was the biggest surprise was the windmill and a pool, in the center of the village. Wally explained to Jimmy that KO had built the windmill so the village could have fresh water year-round without carrying it. KO also ensured every home had all the bowls, plates, tubs, pads, and their favorite, at least one large house mirror. The Sasquatch are not vain, but enjoy seeing themselves and ensuring their fur is clean and smooth.

Wally finally brought Jimmy to his home so he could meet his mother. Lanie had told Jimmy how she met Wally, or Gu as his mother calls him, and he was looking forward to meeting her. When Wally entered his home, he went directly to his mother who was reclining on a pad next to Wally's dad. Wally's mother stood, hugged her big son, then turned to Jimmy with her arms held out to hug him as well. Jimmy stepped right in for a hug. Jimmy wasn't a huge kid, but he wasn't small either. When he hugged Wally's mother, it made him feel like a small boy getting hugged by grandma, in a fur coat.

Wally sat on the floor looking at his dad, and they spoke in Sasquatch using signs and words, and occasionally, they would use a human word, too. Jimmy had been learning Sasquatch and could keep up with most of the conversation but wasn't sure what Wally's father meant about him becoming the leader soon. Wally finished the conversation and hugged his dad and mom, who in turn hugged Jimmy. This time Wally's dad didn't kiss him on the head, but he did ruffle his hair a bit. Wally and Jimmy said goodbye to Wally's troupe as they left, and they were sure to let Jimmy know he was allowed anytime he wanted, even without Gu. Wally told Jimmy; KO was the only other human who was allowed to come into the village unescorted.

After meeting Wally's parents, the boys went outside to say goodbye to the rest of the troupe. The young Sasquatch were excited to meet Jimmy. He was the first human kid they had met. All the Sasquatch troupe met Lanie, Cooper, and KO, but those were adult humans. They could tell Jimmy was a kid and wanted to learn more about him. Once the young Sasquatch's curiosity was satisfied about Jimmy, the boys left the village and headed to Jimmy's boat.

6

WALLY AND JIMMY INTRODUCE NEW SASQUATCH TO THE RIVER PEOPLE

Most people who live along the Tomoka River already knew Wally because of KO. Wally and Jimmy wanted to introduce the people living and working on the river to some of the other Sasquatch in Wally's troupe so that the humans and the Sasquatch could work together. The boys know the humans and Sasquatch can help one another, so they devise a plan.

One by one the boys stopped at the river people's homes along the Tomoka River, throughout the marshes and swamps. Before they stopped at one of the river people's homes, they decided what that river person might need the most as far as help was concerned. Most people along the Tomoka were self-sufficient, but a bit of help never hurt, especially if that helper could pull a fishing boat up onto the drydock without a winch.

Some of the river people ran crab pots, others caught gators, some gathered nuts, and some had small gardens, but they all could use a bit of help sometimes, so Jimmy and Wally set their plan in motion.

The boys picked specific Sasquatch to help each river person.

Some of the taller male Sasquatch loved wading and working crab pots, so the boys introduced the river people who crabbed with those Sasquatch. Most female Sasquatch preferred dry land and helped with the nut gathering and in gardens. The more adventurous younger male Sasquatch enjoyed wrestling the gators, so the boys introduced them to the river people who hunted gators.

Many of the river people would only need a bit of help now and then, so they would have the Sasquatch stop by occasionally to see if the river people needed help.

Many of the adult Sasquatch spoke enough English to communicate with the river people, but the young Sasquatch were the best talkers and enjoyed spending time with humans. Once the river people met and spent time with the Sasquatch, they had no fear of them and truly enjoyed their company. The Sasquatch were always in good moods and enjoyed being around humans. Within a few months, it wasn't uncommon to see river people and Sasquatch sitting on the porch, relaxing or fishing on the dock.

Many of the river people, like Lanie and KO, worked closely with the Sasquatch to ensure they had everything they needed. The Sasquatch adopted the humans into their extended troupe and ensured their favorite humans were protected and cared for as best a Sasquatch can. This means there were no gators, or snakes close to the river people's homes, and the river channels and dirt roads to their homes were always clear.

Wally and Jimmy had succeeded in bringing Humans and Sasquatch together. On the Tomoka, that is. It was going to take quite a while for the rest of the world to be ready for Sasquatch. The boys would work on their little part of the world for now. Wally was beginning to understand he was going to be the leader of his people someday and knew how he wanted to lead. He was going to make sure his people would be safe with the Humans.

7

WALLY AND JIMMY'S ADVENTURES

One of Wally and Jimmy's favorite stories is the night they see a 4X4 truck parked deep in the swamp. Wally and Jimmy were looking for bullfrogs and heard loud music and people laughing. Because of gators, snakes, and panthers, it wasn't normal for humans to be so deep in the swamp, especially at night. Jimmy and Wally decided to investigate in case someone could get hurt. They slowly sneaked through the brush to the truck, and when they reached it, they were mad at what they saw.

There were four people in a big crew cab 4X4 pickup drinking beer and throwing the empties outside onto the ground. To say Wally reacts to littering a bit more aggressively than a normal person or Sasquatch is an understatement. The Sasquatch are clean beings that live off the land and create no pollution. The Sasquatch have always collected what humans lose and even go through their garbage to salvage what they can. The Sasquatch never pollutes and gets angry when humans do. Wally gets angrier than most Sasquatch, maybe because he will be the leader someday and sees the real damage.

Wally was so mad he was going to tip the truck on its side, but Jimmy told him that that could hurt the truck and possibly the people inside, so instead, Wally lifted the back of the truck and placed a log under it, so they couldn't drive away. The driver jumped out of the truck to see what had just happened. One look at Wally, who at this point was standing tall, with his arms reaching for the guy, and then he let out a super loud roar. The driver jumped back into his truck, locked the door, and dove onto the truck floor.

Jimmy later said he couldn't be sure, but Wally said his sense of smell was better, and he was closer, so yes, the guy did mess himself.

Jimmy and Wally stayed by the truck for about 30 minutes, and at no time did anyone step out of the truck, so they left. The truck windows never came back down. They turned the music off and shut all the truck lights off. Jimmy and Wally were staying at the Sasquatch Village a mile from where the truck was log-bound, so they had an easy walk with Wally as the guide, but the nearest human house was 10 miles away. That meant the people in the truck needed to walk 10 miles down a dirt road, surrounded by a swamp filled with snakes, alligators, and panthers at night.

Being that these beer drinkers came out into the swamp in a 4X4 crew cab pickup, Wally and Jimmy assumed they didn't have any flashlights, so they were going to wait until daylight before they tried heading out of the swamp. Since they weren't worried the people in the truck might try to leave at night, the boys went back to Wally's village for the night.

Wally and Jimmy walked back to the truck the next morning to see what was happening. When they got to the truck, there were no humans around. It had been light for a few hours, so the boys figured the driver and passengers walked back at first light. Wally was laughing at what it must have been like for them to stay in the truck all night, terrified about the huge beast outside. Jimmy told Wally he had a cold heart and then started laughing as well.

After Jimmy and Wally made sure there weren't any humans left with the truck, they picked up all the beer cans and threw them into the truck. Wally wrote do not litter on the side of the truck with mud, then lifted the truck off the log so that it could drive away like nothing happened. Jimmy and Wally wanted the driver to get into trouble for lying about the truck being stuck on a log and having everyone walk home. So Wally moved the log, and now it would appear that the driver was too drunk to drive and thought he was stuck.

Jimmy and Wally returned to Wally's village and headed out for the day. Later that day, they returned to the truck, and it was gone. Jimmy never heard a thing about the truck or the occupants being scared by a monster. He thought the driver might have been too young to be drinking and had gotten in trouble when he got home. Who would believe his story of a monster picking up his truck and putting a log under it if the driver and passengers had been drinking? Maybe the kid had his friends drive them back out to get the truck, but whatever they did, no story of a monster in the swamp was told. No matter what happened afterward, they had to hike 10 miles to get home, so a lesson might have been learned.

8

WALLY PLAYS FOOTBALL

Jimmy was up early preparing for his high school's homecoming football game followed by the dance that night. He needed to get his chores done and return home in time to get cleaned up. He and Wally had some fish deliveries to take care of, and afterwards Jimmy was going to show Wally where he could watch the game from tonight. Wally knew Jimmy played football and had seen a few games on TV, but had never seen a football game in person, so they decided to find a spot Wally could sneak into to watch. Jimmy found a good hiding spot under the grandstands on top of the men's locker room.

The back of the locker room was 10 feet away from the thick swamp brush, and Wally could easily walk through the swamp, climb on top of the locker room, and watch the game hiding behind the roof equipment. There was a large grating to allow air to flow into the HVAC equipment on the locker room roof that Wally could watch the game through. Jimmy and Wally decided it would be best to get Wally there early so no one would see him. Once Jimmy was ready, he headed out to get Wally.

Jimmy loaded the boat with an extra gas tank because today they were going to do their runs nonstop, so they could be done in time to get ready for the game. It was on the second stop when Jimmy called his friend, his football team's center, to see if his family wanted their fish that day, when he heard the bad news. His friend, the team's star center, was sick. He and Wally dropped their plans and headed up the river to go see the sick center. Jimmy dropped Wally off on the shore just before they reached the center's house so no one would see Wally. Jimmy tied up his boat and went to the house.

Jimmy let himself in and went to his friend's room. His friend said he was really sick and couldn't play that night. His parents were gone through the weekend, so he would stay here. Jimmy realized only then that the only one who knew the center was sick was him. He had a plan, and he needed to introduce Wally to his friend to save the game.

Jimmy looked at his friend and said, "If you don't play today, we lose, and you may not get the scholarship you want, right?"

"I thought about that, but I am so sick I can barely walk to the bathroom, so there is no way I can play, which means my dreams die today!"

"How about you and I do something that saves the game, your scholarship, and will be super fun?" asked Jimmy.

"I am not sure how you plan to do that, but I am more than willing to try anything to save the game and my scholarship," said the center.

"I will be back in 5 minutes with my friend."

Jimmy walked to the river shore and called for Wally to come to him. Jimmy knew that Wally could walk through the dense brush much faster than he could get in the boat drive, and drive back. They like to show off how big and strong they were anyway. Wally never tired of reminding Jimmy how small he was and how often he needed Wally's help. If it weren't true, Jimmy would be upset but absolutely appreciated Wally's help. Tonight, he was going to find out how much Wally appreciated helping. Sure enough, Wally came stomping out of the brush with a big smile because he knew he'd just saved Jimmy a lot of time and effort not having to drive his boat to pick him up. Jimmy sometimes fed him guff, but Wally had picked him up and carried him on his shoulders through some rough, thick brush so many times Jimmy couldn't count on his fingers.

Jimmy shook his head at Wally and said, "Always a big show off." Then he laughed.

"Not show off, just can do!" Said Wally triumphantly.

"I think I have something you might like to do," said Jimmy. "it involves getting dressed up and pretending to be a human, playing football, helping us win our game, and making sure my friend doesn't lose his scholarship." Jimmy added.

"I don't know what a scholarship is," said Wally, "but I want to play football, and it will be fun dressing up as a puny human," he added, breaking up laughing until they got to the door.

Jimmy quickly explained to Wally what he planned to do and that this was the first time his friend had seen a Sasquatch, so he needed to be careful. Wally had met plenty of humans and knew that his looks and size were intimidating to humans, so he always tried to act gentle and move slowly when he met humans for the first time.

Jimmy went in first so he could explain to his friend that he would be bringing Wally in. He then explained that Wally was over 7 feet tall, weighed over 400 pounds and basically looked like a large gorilla.

His friend at the team's center said, "he was sick, not stupid or crazy, so for Jimmy to go home and leave him alone so he could rest."

"Well, looks like I have to break out the big guns, or more like the big apes, to show you," said Jimmy, then he left the bedroom, went out, opened the front door, and let Wally in.

Now Jimmy's friend is big, but nothing compared to Wally, so when he returned to his friend's bedroom door, he walked in first, warned that this new friend looked a bit scary, but was friendly, then stepped aside, and Wally came in. Well, Wally ducked to get in the doorway. It was a good thing the sick center was lying in bed when Wally came in, otherwise he would have run away screaming. As it was, he was pushed up hard against his headboard, mouth opened like he was screaming, but he was scared silent.

Jimmy and Wally began laughing immediately because the big tough center had pulled the covers over his head and was hiding like a scared kid. Like hiding under covers was going to protect him from something as big as Wally. It took almost a minute of Jimmy and Wally's laughing for the sick center to peek out from under the covers. When he finally did, he saw Jimmy and the big hairy ape on the floor, holding onto one another, laughing so hard they were crying.

It was as much embarrassment as a curiosity that allowed the center to come out from under the covers and look at the two laughing nuts on the floor. The sight of his friend Jimmy and a giant ape hugging one another and laughing caused the football center to start laughing also because as scary as the ape looked, he could tell he was friendly. When the three teen boys had stopped laughing enough, Jimmy and Wally stood so they could begin making introductions. The center got out of bed so that he could stand next to Wally, held out his hand, and said, "Hi, I'm Jake. What's your name?"

Wally looked down at Jake and said, "Hi Jake. I am Wally."

After Wally introduced himself, Jake just kept staring wide-eyed and open-mouthed, thinking to himself how unbelievable it was that this giant ape could actually talk, and he was still hoping it wouldn't eat him either.

Jimmy entered the room, put his arm around Wally, and asked, "So do you like your replacement for tonight?"

Jake shook off his open mouth stare, looked at Jimmy, and asked, "Are you serious?" "You want to replace me with a giant monkey?" He added.

Wally wasn't hurt or offended by Jake's monkey comment, but he pretended he was when someone said something insensitive like that, so he leaned towards Jake and let out a long, deep growl.

Jake instantly jumped back and said, "I'm sorry, don't eat me!" Then he cowered against the wall.

Jimmy jokingly said, "No, no, no bad Sasquatch, don't eat the scared boy." Then he and Wally began laughing out of control again.

Jake realized he'd been teased, looked at the two laughing idiots across from him, and also began laughing. When they settled down and had been given real introductions, Jimmy explained his plan.

The team needed to win the game tonight because it was the homecoming game, and that meant team honor was at stake. Second, the dance would be a bust if they lost the game; everyone in the school would be disappointed, and the team would feel even worse. Lastly, and the most important thing to Jake was that if he didn't play tonight, he might lose the college scholarship he hoped for. Wally was going to have to play for Jake tonight and save the game.

Jimmy explained further that the game was going to be played on a rare cold winter night in Florida. The game time temperature was going to be near freezing, so there could be rain and sleet, which meant many of the kids would be wearing face masks and gloves. Jimmy suggested if Wally slouched a bit, he would be almost the same height as Jake, so the facemask would hide his real identity.

It took a little bit of shaving on Wally's face so that no fur stuck out of the mask. And by 'a little bit' of shaving, means they went through 2 of Jake's dad's blades shaving his face. Wally thought he looked more like a human than ever and might not need the mask until Jimmy suggested he smile and look into the mirror. One look and Wally agreed that even his smile looked like he was going to bite someone. Wally has teeth much like a gorilla's when he smiles. He has huge canine fangs that are more for show than to go with his nice temperament. He could easily use his teeth to defend himself, but he was so big that nothing in the swamp could hurt him.

Even though Jake had a custom helmet made to fit his oversized head, there was no way to make the helmet fit Wally's bigger head without removing the protective pads. Being boys, it never dawned on them what the protective pads were there for or that Wally could have gotten hurt without them. Although it should be noted that Wally could head butt a tree, knock it down, and not get hurt, so no mere high school boy could possibly inflict damage to Wally's head with theirs.

Even with the pads removed, Wally cracked the helmet down the center seam in the back. When he pulled it on, his head was so big. The helmet was now ruined, but at least it fit Wally's head. Jake was one of the biggest high school players at 6-foot-8-inch tall, 340 pounds, so Wally's 7-foot-2inch, 400 pounds wasn't too big of a difference, at least Jimmy thought.

Wally barely fit into the football jersey, even without the shoulder pads. Neither Jake nor Jimmy could tell Wally wasn't wearing shoulder pads. His shoulders were so big. Wally was only 14 years old, but he was easily as strong as four human adult male professional football players. Wally had been around humans since he was five years old, so he knew to use care when playing or working with humans. For Wally, playing football with high school boys would be the equivalent of an adult male playing football with 7-year-old boys. Wally was going to have fun, but he also needed to be careful not to hurt the others.

The pants fit ok, but there was no way Wally could wear pads in them also. Luckily Wally's muscles bulged out, and with the fur, it looked like he was wearing pads. 'If you squinted,' said Jake. The biggest problem after the shaving fiasco was trying to find shoes for Wally. The nickname Bigfoot was given to the Sasquatch for a reason.

The boys couldn't find any shoes that fit Wally, no matter where they looked. Wally's foot was almost half longer and wider than Jake's, and Jake wore a size 18. After trying everything else, they decided to shave Wally's feet and paint them to look like shoes.

Jimmy said the game was going to be at night. It was raining and maybe sleeting off and on, the football field lights weren't that good in the rain, and the field was muddy, so all the players had dirty shoes. Jimmy was sure they had thought of everything.

To say the game was a blowout would be an understatement. Not only could Wally easily hold the whole front line by himself after he hiked the ball, but it turns out Sasquatch are fast, too. Wally picked up a fumble, and everyone yelled to run, so he ran the ball for a touchdown. While he ran for a touchdown, he was pulling three of the other team's players like they weren't there.

After the game, everyone rushed onto the field and congratulated Wally, who they all thought was Jake. Even the coach was beside himself. Everyone was so excited about the team winning the game and Jake's fantastic performance that no one noticed Jake had grown over 6 inches. Even his own dad came up and hugged him and didn't notice. It is good that the weather was so bad and everything and everybody was wet and cold because no one wanted to stay on the field too long.

Wally kept quiet and accepted the attention, then Jimmy came to his rescue and said he was taking Jake home because he was feeling tired after putting out so hard. No one argued because they all wanted to go warm up and get to the dance. Jimmy led Wally, dressed as a wet, tired Jake, to his car.

The real Jake met them in Jimmy's car. Jake was feeling well enough by game time. He snuck to the game and onto the top of the gym where Wally was supposed to hide and watch the whole game, then snuck into Jimmy's car to wait. Jimmy drove Wally, still dressed as Jake in the football uniform with Jake to Jake's house, and the three had a blast talking about the game.

After Wally's unhuman performance, dressed as Jake on the field that night, Jake received the scholarship he wanted and a few unexpected ones. A few years later, the football scouts said Jake never played quite as well as he did that night, but he still made it into the pros.

9

LIFE GROWING UP ON THE RIVER

Jimmy grew up on the Halifax and Tomoka rivers and had many funny experiences that couldn't happen these days with cell phones and cameras.

Jimmy's house was on the river, and he used to drive his boat across the Halifax River to go to school. Once across, he would tie his boat up to his dad's friend, Mr. Thompson's dock, and walk to school. Sometimes, the water was too rough to make it across, so he missed school. Sometimes he would get to the other side, tie up to the dock, and hide until the owner left for work, and then head out to go fishing. Fishing was becoming more important to Jimmy than school.

Jimmy and his friends took a long lunch break during school one sunny day. On a whim, he took the few friends out in his boat. Everything was going fine until they came upon a tide buoy with steps, and one of his friends decided to climb onto it. Of course, Jimmy and the other friends backed the boat up and left him on the buoy in the middle of the Halifax River for 30 minutes or so. In those days, no one had cell phones, and it was a weekday, so no one was on the river to help his friend.

When they finally returned to get him, he was wet past his knees. When they got back to school, the boy's shoes made squishing noises as he walked down the hall. It is a memory that Jimmy will keep forever, and they were grateful they didn't have phones and cameras, so they never got in trouble.

Then, there were the times Jimmy got into trouble when he was out in the boat fishing. Many times, a storm would suddenly appear and catch him off guard. In those days, there weren't hundreds of weather channels, and Jimmy didn't have a radio, so if a coastal storm came up without warning, it could cause problems.

More than once, during a surprise storm that came with a tide surge, Jimmy was caught on the wrong side of a bridge and needed to get to the other side to get home to safety. There were a few close calls, but there was one time in particular when the water was too high to get the boat under the bridge. The storm had quickly become worse, and the boat was so tall with the tower that it would have been badly damaged, or they might have gotten hurt if they tried to go under the bridge.

Their only option was to take the tower off the boat to get under the bridge. Jimmy could barely keep the boat under control as the storm became stronger and the waves higher. Wally almost fell in more than once, but with his superior strength, he got the tower off the boat, and they were low enough to make it under the bridge.

The sad part was there were many places Wally couldn't go in the boat with Jimmy, like the old marinas and bait shacks. The old timers wouldn't have taken kindly to having a giant ape walk into their store and scaring all the customers. Jimmy went to those kinds of places alone, and that is how he learned all he knew about fishing. The old timers back in the 1960s and 1970s loved teaching the youngsters all they knew so all their skills wouldn't be lost. Truth be told, the old timers loved to talk to anybody that would listen, which is why they spent their days at the dock fishing and socializing.

10

WALLY AND JIMMY WORK WITH THE SASQUATCH

Jimmy caught the fishing bug early, and it became a passion, so by the time he turned 18, he had saved enough money, and he was old enough, and so he bought his own commercial fishing boat. He didn't want any help from his parents, or his dad would have insisted on inspecting the boat, and helping Jimmy when he was fishing. Jimmy steadfastly said he didn't want help and wanted to be a success, but by his own hands. He didn't dare tell his dad he had a Sasquatch as a best friend and fishing partner.

In the beginning Jimmy and Wally went out fishing together. It soon became obvious that it would be impossible to hide Wally on a regular fishing boat. The average full-grown adult male Sasquatch was generally around 8 feet tall. Wally was now 15 years old and almost 9 feet tall. If Wally was going to ride in the boat, he had to do it sitting on the boat deck so he wasn't so tall. Most of the time, if Jimmy took a Sasquatch out fishing, it was one of the other young Sasquatch, who wasn't as tall as Wally.

Once Jimmy could find an outlet for the fish he caught, he

d have
become a Sasquatch favorite. The Sasquatch would sometimes
help by bringing the catches to KO's marina to pick up and sell
them.

The Sasquatch were happy to help, and many began eating
fish like Wally did. KO always says the fish and great food he fed
Wally when he was a baby caused him to grow so big. Now the
other Sasquatch wanted to eat fish, hoping they, too, could grow.
The Sasquatch incredible strength made hauling in the fishing
gear much easier. All the fishing boat deck hands wore floatation
bibs and hats, including the Sasquatch, so they looked like a
normal fisherman from a distance. The problem was the average
Sasquatch were 2-feet taller than the average human fisherman.
Jimmy and Cooper made a special boat deck with a 2-foot-deep
trough next to the side of the boat, so a Sasquatch could stand in
the boat and not look taller than a human. When humans were
working on these boats, they had to use care so they didn't fall into
the Sasquatch troughs.

The Sasquatch is especially helpful when it is time to haul
boats out. The Sasquatch can't swim because of their weight, but
they are great shore and dock help, plus they work for peanuts.
Seriously, the Sasquatch work for peanuts, which they prefer over

40

money, because they can eat the peanuts and have no need for money.

Over the years, more people have learned about Wally and his Sasquatch troupe, but Jimmy and the other friends of the Sasquatch try to keep their knowledge of them as quiet as possible. The last thing the Sasquatch or river people needed was to have some government agencies come snooping around, and then the rest of the world would find out about them. The river people wanted their privacy, as did the Sasquatch, so everyone worked to keep their secret safe.

11

JIMMY MEETS LOIS

In the mid-1980s, Jimmy was visiting KO at his Tomoka marina when Wally came by and asked them to accompany him to meet someone. KO and Jimmy asked where they were going, but Wally told them it was a surprise. KO looked at Jimmy and said he was up for an adventure if he was. Jimmy shrugged his shoulders and told Wally to lead the way. Wally smiled, turned, and walked out of the marina, under the bridge, over to the railroad tracks, and headed East alongside the tracks.

The Sasquatch used the railroad tracks to travel around whenever possible. The tracks are faster and easier than pushing through the dense brush, plus, having to walk a ways down the tracks to reach a trail keeps the Sasquatch trails further from where humans might find them. Wally didn't say a word while they walked, but he was smiling big, and Jimmy wasn't sure what was up. After about a mile of walking along the railroad tracks, Wally turned onto a well-worn trail without saying a word. KO whispered that Wally seemed proud he was about to surprise us just as they walked into a clearing with a pool in the center.

The pool was clear and in the center of a clearing, set in the middle of a very dense jungle. On the opposite side of the clearing from the trail they just came in on was a small cottage with a deck. On the deck was a lady playing a piano. Surrounding the deck was half of Wally's troupe, laying around and listening. There really isn't a weirder scene than a bunch of Sasquatch lounging around a pond in the middle of the jungle, listening to a lady play piano. Jimmy and KO stared at the impossibly silly sight for a few seconds until the lady saw them and stopped playing.

The lady stood up and walked towards them. As the lady approached, she smiled deeply at Wally and when they met, he bent down and hugged her. Wally was now 10 feet tall and 1200 pounds, and he was bending down to hug a 5-foot-6-inch lady, which was a sight. After the two hugged one another, Wally introduced Jimmy and KO to her.

Wally explained he had met Lois a year ago after hearing her play her piano. He wanted to wait until she was settled before he introduced her to the rest of the friends of the Sasquatch. Wally explained how she made this a safe spot for the Sasquatch to come. Jimmy and KO spent the afternoon learning about Lois and the small group of seniors who lived in the Bear Creek Community, who also helped the Sasquatch. Before they left, KO and Jimmy promised Lois they would visit again, and they were glad Wally had such great friends. KO told Lois she could come by his marina anytime and go fishing. Lois said she would enjoy it, and maybe Gu would walk her down sometime soon.

Wally and Jimmy spent as much time together as possible while the years passed by. Wally became the leader of all the Sasquatch troupes within a 100-mile radius. He was almost 2 feet taller than any other Sasquatch, and his knowledge of humans made him the perfect choice for the Sasquatch to have a safe future. Jimmy spent all his time fishing, finally owning many boats, a fish market, and a restaurant. I bet if you looked at the menu in Jimmy's restaurant, it would have blueberry hush puppies and blue crab.

Jimmy and Wally are still great friends and can still be seen some nights fishing the Tomoka, reminiscing the wonderful years gone by, and eating blueberry hush puppies.

ABOUT THE AUTHOR

Patrick Talmadge Sr. has always been a late bloomer. His growth didn't cease until he was over 21 years old. He reached his pinnacle as a national and world-class masters middle-distance runner at the age of 37, when he won his first master's national track and field championship in the 800-meter run.

At 47, Patrick earned his Bachelor of Arts degree and made history as the oldest NCAA cross-country runner. Seven years later, at 54, he returned to college to pursue a Master's degree in Psychology. During this time, he ran the mile in track, once again setting a record as the oldest NCAA track and field runner. He received his Master's degree in Psychology at 57. At the age of 66, he embarked on his writing journey.

Patrick taught himself to read at the tender age of three and a half and has been an avid reader ever since. With a keen interest in all fields of science, science fiction, and fantasy, he amassed a wealth of knowledge that would later prove invaluable when he began writing. Throughout his 20s and 30s, Patrick devoured two to three books a day. Upon graduating from graduate school in 2011, he retired from competitive running and felt a growing desire to write the stories that had been simmering within him.

In November 2021, spurred on by the love of his life, Patrick began his writing career. By July 2023, he had completed an adult four-book science fiction series about Sasquatch, a four-book children's series on the same subject, and a standalone novel about a senior community that befriends a troupe of Sasquatch.

Patrick possesses a unique ability to write multiple stories simultaneously, allowing him to modify and adjust interconnected narratives for clarity when writing a series. With a bit of luck, Patrick will continue to pursue his passion for writing for the rest of his life, or at least until his computer gives out.

ALSO BY PATRICK TALMADGE

AFTERWORD

Go to hangarıpublishing.com to learn more about the Authors and stay up to date with their newest releases.

www.ingramcontent.com/pod-product-compliance
Lightning Source LLC
Chambersburg PA
CBHW071545120626
46550CB00006B/2587